Newborn

KATE CLANCHY was born in Glasgow in 1965 and was educated in Edinburgh and Oxford. Her two previous poetry collections, *Slattern* (1996) and *Samarkand* (1999), brought her many literary awards including a Somerset Maugham award and Saltire and Forward Prizes. She lives in Oxford with her family and works as a teacher, writer and broadcaster.

KATE CLANCHY

Newborn

PICADOR

First published 2004 by Picador
an imprint of Pan Macmillan Ltd
Pan Macmillan, 20 New Wharf Road, London N1 9RR
Basingstoke and Oxford
Associated companies throughout the world
www.panmacmillan.com

ISBN 0 330 41930 7

A CIP catalogue record for this book is available from
the British Library.

Typeset by Pan Macmillan Design deartment
Printed and bound in Great Britain by
Mackays of Chatham plc, Chatham, Kent

For M.O.C.R.

Acknowledgements

Some of these poems first appeared in the *Guardian*, *Poetry Review*, and *Magma*, and were broadcast on BBC Radio 3 and 4.

This text has benefitted from the attention of Matthew Reynolds, Colette Bryce and Don Paterson.

I am grateful for the financial support of The Arts Council of England.

Contents

One, Two

The camera has caught me
in a church doorway, stooping
to fasten what must be

my old cork-soled sandals,
their thick suede straps,
that dry, worn grip at heel

and instep. I'm smiling
downwards, pinkly
self-conscious, and above me

the arch is an extraordinary
blue. New – the whole place
was just lime-washed, azure

and sapphire rough-brushed
over moss. It stood in the moist heat
at a confluence of rivers –

I've even noted their names,
and the date, which says you, love,
are perhaps ten cells old.

In the humid space beneath
my dress, my body is bent
in the small effort of buckling,

the sag of my stomach briefly
leant on my thigh,
and, at the crux, in the press

of my nerveless places, you
are putting me on, easily,
the way a foot puts on a shoe.

Two Months Gone

It makes us want to shut all doors,
turn off the news, the phone, light
after light, pull the stairs, like a ladder,
up behind us, until, beneath the covers,
the darkness pressing in around us,

we are the pair in the heart of the tale,
the woodsman who spared the unicorn,
the kitchen maid who hooked a witch
from the well and held her toe
through fourteen frightful incarnations,

and won, walked home with a wish
like a brimming glass of water, and when
the goblin with the question came,
sang out, to his single rhymed conundrum,
the answer: *all we ever wanted.*

In the black after the thunderclap, we wait
for the crooked town to wake, find
gilded roofs, loaves on each table,
for the crowds to come, half-dressed, incredulous,
for our fortune, squalling in its cradle.

Undercurrent

I see them at every corner, now,
babies' hands, their bobbing feet,
pointing always other
to the flow of the street:

flotsam in a harbour, marking
where a tide
is running strongly contrariwise.

Scan

They showed me on the screen
some star lit hills, a lucky sky,
then, resting among haar-filled fields,

a settlement round the outlet
of a phosphorescent river, all low windows
flickering with early electricity.

And they pointed out with a line of light
a hub like the start of a knotting city,
like a storm in a weather front, coalescing.

Under Weigh

In the last month I would cycle
each dusk round the meadow,
watching the rabbits hop briskly
away from the wheel. This was May
and the hay grew knee-high, thigh-
high, and I scythed through it – past
whippets and walkers, slender,
meandering lovers – thinking
of the physics of ships, how a keel
cuts best through deep waters
under a certain pressure of freight.

Pang

Forget the last weeks beached
in Joanna's garden watching
the snails gluily labour
up the inside arch of the trellis
and smash from the apex
eight feet to the ground, also
the dirt taste of raspberry-leaf tea.

You came for me early, like a keen
first date, announcing yourself
with an eager, even over-familiar,
uncle-ish hard tweak at my waist.

Driving to the Hospital

We were low on petrol
so I said let's freewheel
when we get to the hill.
It was dawn and the city
was nursing its quiet
and I liked the idea
of arriving with barely
a crunch on the gravel.
You smiled kindly and
eased the clutch gently
and backed us out of
the driveway and patted
my knee with exactly
the gesture you used
when we were courting,
remember, on the way
to your brother's: *I like
driving with my baby,*
that's what you said. And
at the time I wondered
why my heart leapt and leapt.

I had my eyes shut the whole time

and in that inner cinema saw
the ruched vermilion curtains rise
on a vast screen showing lava. There,
you issued forth in scarlet flumes,
in cinescope, in a sunrise of burst veins.

What Can I Say

Like the Japanese tricks
you could buy for twopence
those tight lacquer seeds
which uncurled in water
then bloomed into red
tissue flowers, algal, alarming;
or those cellophane fish
that twitched on your palm
for 'fever' or 'lust'; like
those shit-coils of sand
a razor-fish shoots out
when it sink-drills itself
back to wet salt and you think
how can a shelled thing
be so fast and afraid: like
all things unfolding, tumbling
suddenly, catkins, fishing nets,
mainsails, sheets, like
the reel's hectic spooling
when the salmon is hooked,
like a parachute abruptly
uncrushing, blooming
to skull-shape, jerking you
upright with that familiar crack:

this opening up of a person,
this bringing the new person out.

Driving Home

I want you to know
it was your father
picked you up when
you were crumpled
and warm as a handkerchief
drawn from his pocket,
and your father who walked
you out of the maze
of the hospital while I
flapped largely behind,
and your father who
tucked you into the car
and chose the exit
unerringly and drove
us home evenly, slowly
as though we were nosing
through floral, curious
crowds, as if the car
were an Ambassador
and we were rich
suddenly, tremulous, old.

Love

I hadn't met his kind before.
His misericord face – really
like a joke on his father – blurred
as if from years of polish;
his hands like curled dry leaves;

the profligate heat he gave
out, gave out, his shallow,
careful breaths: I thought
his filaments would blow,
I thought he was an emperor,

dying on silk cushions.
I didn't know how to keep
him wrapped, I didn't know
how to give him suck, I had
no idea about him. At night

I tried to remember the feel
of his head on my neck, the skull
small as a cat's, the soft spot
hot as a smelted coin,
and the hair, the down, fine

as the innermost, vellum layer
of some rare snowcreature's
aureole of fur, if you could meet
such a beast, if you could
get so near. I started there.

Infant

In your frowning, fugitive days, small love,
your coracled, ecstatic nights,
possessed or at peace, hands clenched
on an unseen rope, or raised in blessing
like the Pope, as your white etched feet
tread sooty roofs of canal tunnels
or lie released, stretched north in sleep –

you seem to me an early saint, a Celt,
eyes fixed on a celestial light, patiently
setting the sextant straight
to follow your godsent map, now
braced against a baffling gale, now
becalmed, fingers barely sculling
through warm muddy tides.

Soon, you will make your way out
of this estuary country, leave
the low farms and fog banks, tack through
the brackish channels and long
reed-clogged rivulets, reach
the last turn, the salt air and river mouth,
the wide grey sea beyond it.

When You Cried

I sat and mourned, let you
thrash on my lap like a choking fish.
The way your soft spine
chain-linked, grew strong!

It was as if you were a salmon
and our arms were nets, as if
you were searching upstream,
upstream, for the dark pool

you came from, for your
proper ground. I thought
you'd seen through us, that
you knew this wasn't home.

Rejoice in the Lamb

At night, in your shift, fine hair upright,
you are my tiny Bedlamite,
admonishing the laughing crowd
with your pale, magisterial hands,
or roaring out like poor Kit Smart
how blessed, electric, all things are.

On Breast-Feeding,

of which I am strongly in favour,
in the same way as when I visited China
and walked down the Ceremonial Road
where formerly only the Emperor
(or Emperor and Procession: eunuchs,
closed litters of chrysanthemum silk)
walked once a year on the winter solstice,
past the shut shutters and frozen hush
of the entire interdicted populace; when I,
on a merely touristic visit, walked
this sacred road to the Round Altar
of the Temple of Heaven (which is round
in itself, the Temple, round after round
of glazed blue roof ascending), when I
clambered up the glittering tiers of the three
concentric alabaster terraces and stood
at the top in the innermost circle, on the spot
which once held the Throne of Heaven,
which marked the centre of everything,
the very middle of the Middle
(or should we say central?) Kingdom,
when I did this not alone, but with crowds,
with Chinese in their hundreds, with
tour groups, students and families all
laughing, all joshing, all testing the echoes,
all posing for photos, everywhere
but above all on that central spot, on
the site where, for five centuries, only
the Emperor had ever stood (the Emperor,

tasting the dust of the solstice, observing
the ranks of silent silk rumps), when
I saw instead people dashing to beat
the self-timer, families in nuclear
and extended formations, troupes
in uniforms, miniskirts, yellow tour T-shirts,
in apparently ironic Mao badges and caps –

I was strongly in favour of that.

The Burden

I'd never have thought that this would be me,
content to tote the baby homewards
answering, rook-like, his hoarse calls,
counting the haws on the bare claw branches,
the rose hips shining like blood.

And you'd be the one at the gate left staring
at the cloud-shadows etched on the copper water,
the flooded fields we couldn't cross.
That I'd let a hundred yards stretch between us.
How bright this thin, bisected moon.

Silt

The floods have come to Angel Meadow.
Yesterday I raced the pram
over the soaked sedimented turf
till the baby gave his harsh pleased caw –

now our silver tracks are all
rubbed out, and the playground
is a pewter plate, and the trees
have thrown their last leaves on it.

The willows toss their heads
like pettish girls. You'd think
they'd be used to things like this,
on this ancient, sunk, flood meadow.

The clouds are black, fat, move
across us much too fast.
The baby holds up both his hands,
certain he can catch them.

Aneurysm

When my father heard his friend
was dead, we sat a while and talked
of traffic: how cars clog
each by-way now, every road
you think you know. We were quiet,
and I lit the lamp. I thought

I could hear the cars outside,
bashing, lowing, rank on rank.
There'd been a crash, my father said,
and his friend had walked out,
shaken, saved. It was hours
before the blood-clot got him.

I held my baby on my lap. It was
dark, it was the winter solstice.
We said there is no such thing
as the right route or a clear passage
no matter where you start,
or how you plan it.

Plain Work

We should knit, Joanna,
or tat, however that is done.
These winter afternoons –
we should drop wood eggs
down socks, or hold
long knotted wefts between us.

We should have stuff
to show for this: for the days
we've sat together, waiting
for our babies to get over
a tooth, a want, a croupy fever;
to get an hour older.

Yards of it by now – enough
to fill this room, surround us.
Great rolls of random rainbow
cloth, twisted, lumpen, fine,
the bright wool stitched in,
stitched in, line by line.

Not Art

This is close work, this babystuff,
the intricate wiping and wrapping, the slow
unpicking of miniature fists;
village-work, a hand-craft, all bodges
and spit, the gains inchingly small
as the knotting of carpets, raw wool
rasping in the teeth of the comb.

The strewing and stooping, the prising
of muck from the grain of the floor –
I think of gleaners, ash-sifters, of tents
sewn with shoe soles, wedding veils, plaits,
how patchwork is stitched-up detritus,
how it circles on quilts like the bits
of a house in a typhoon's trail.

And the ache in the neck, in the back,
in the foot, are the knocks of wood looms,
narrow as cradles, borne from pasture
to valley to camp. I am learning
the art of mistakes, to accept
every evening that the marks of the day
are woven in too far back to pick out.

This is the work women draw from the river,
wet to the waist, singing in time,
the work we swing from our shoulders,
lay on the ground and let the crowd
hold and finger and weigh up – the young girls
wondering, the laughing old women,
the halt, the milk-eyed, the blind.

Ararat

Winter of floods – winter of broken banks
and radio warnings and me running
down the road with the pushchair screaming
and a cloud helicoptering low behind me.

Remember even the genteel Cherwell
bursting, the Isis brimming, swelling under
its muddy meniscus like a body rolling
in sleep in a blanket? The times you came home

to find the armchairs floating, the carpet
a quicksand, the tables at unprecedented levels,
the baby awash in his Moses basket and me
bailing madly as he rose to the ceiling?

Yet here we all are, no worse than muddy, and look –
the hills emerging, exactly the same, casual as knees.

Find

When he's at his grandparents'
we can't sleep without him
rolled in his blankets,
two floors below us:

the heart of the house,
muscular, unconscious;
deep in our wrappings
our golden scarab.

Learning to Walk

He's on the brink – all day
hanging on a table's edge,
nosing his feet – his fists – his grand
round *Sèvres* head, slowly
into nothing.

           All my life
I've smashed cups and wept,
and this is forever too, I guess;
this liquid heart, this sense
that he's the water, I'm the glass.

In a Prospect of Flowers

So he can walk. We follow
his little trolley out
across the greening garden,

and hope he'll always learn
like this: the random
swipe of feet firming

over months and weeks
to these determined
stiff short steps. Next,

we'd have him sing, or paint,
or play – trumpet, violin –
not scales, you understand, but

jazz, the stuff cut off from us,
so schooled, well-versed . . .
Look out! He's making off.

You go before to sweep the way,
I bend in his mower's wake.
His brahmin's pace. Our scholars' gait.

Storm

So, here
at the height
of this summer
of wrong, in this wrong
hour of this most wrong day
in the heart of the week which went
awry, now while the rain washes
the window free of every
roof we know, of every
tree, you and I, small
one, have come
to an impasse.

You're red,
half-dressed, push-
ing your car up the hill
of the chair. I'm white, flatout
in a field of trousers, listening
to the wind – which is your own twin,
darling – howl for its place, for
its proper season, and bash
our doors and walls
with its enormous
kitchen roll tube
trumpet.

The View

So much of this is cowpoke work,
so much of this is gates and getting
through them – there could be a mountain
rearing above us, there could be a city
hung above the cloudline and still
I'd be keeping my eyes on your footprints,
still I'd be steering this flock home.

Do you think there is a mountain,
my darling, my poppet, stooped there
on your stick like the village elder?
Is it upside down in the depths
of that puddle? I shall flop down
beside you, straight-legged and muddy,
stir up a sunset in the altering oil.

Commonplace

What can I tell you about all this?
After all we are ordinary, and surely
you've seen us, in the park, by
the lake – daily, we watch the swans,
yearlings, come in their dozens,
pale-beaked, identical, throw
them our bread again and again.

What need I say when of course
you remember these long days
going forward, these gold days
sliced lengthways: in the distance
the sound of a train retreating,
the soundless swans turning on the dark
glossy water, the low steps home.

I have nothing to say and will say
anyway: we are commonplace,
he and I, we are borderless, glorious,
we are mother and child coming
home together, and we walk
on fields as green as any field,
babbling like Falstaff when he died.

Rhymes for September

Your wrist sticks an inch from this spring's sweater
as you pick the first curled leaf from the water.
And the turn-ups on your trousers are two turns shorter,
and the sun's sunk to some kind of bathchair
angle, and a cat's-paw breeze is riffling my paper,

flipping the dateline over and over. Where are
they now, our gold afternoons at the lido? This year
I meant to wax them over, store the picture
of us in pellucid water, two akimbo flies in amber,
all winter in the soot of my mind's cellar.

But only last night, now I come to remember,
I heard the boy next door start his meander
up the first four notes of a new trumpet air.
It was *When the Saints* all spring and summer,
now it's *How Many Roads?* And there's my answer.

Dark, Dark

He is calling down the night,
the way he calls out
next door's dog and sees
the word grow ears
and eyes, emerge on heavy
loping legs, a furry
manifest of name.

The dark will have
a lion's neck. He'll ride
its muscled back all night.

Moon, O Moon!

The heaps of leaves he loved
are gone. Now we have
the moon: its thumbprint
on noon airmail skies;
its bitten coin in the night;
its party lantern in the morning,
hungover in the trees.

My metaphors approximate
the sphere
of his apostrophes.

Rain

Did he think words
were things – birds
that would rush to his naming,
hear only his call
in the whole blue sky?

There's no telling. He whines
for a biscuit. He points
to things in books,
mutely as if saying, This too
I have lost. He's been

playing for an hour
with a doll, silently
wadding it into a blanket,
stuffing it into the grate:
and to compound things,

it is raining. He wraps
and wraps the doll's felt
limbs. We watch the shapes
the raindrops make
when they hit the window hard.

Our Balloon

I'm drawing
a hot-air balloon.
A canopy with felt-pen
stripes, a scratchy pencilled
basket. He says it must have
people in it, so I put him in, two
dots, a grin, and since he goes
nowhere solo, add his father
as a beard, myself as curls,
and on request and out
of scale the cat's two
ears and one
stroke
tail.

There.
He stares.
I think

about balloons:
the roar up there,
the chills, the helpless
mild boredom. Do you talk?
I think you can't. I think you
must shade your eyes and mime
towards some house, some farm
shrunk to a diagram, and shout
to the wind, '—onderful time.'
Us in balloon, he says. We are.
It is. And since he'll not
be parted from it,
I fold
up

his balloon
and tuck it
in his pocket.

The Dream of Warm Things

All the way back he talks about
the calf we saw in the field,
a Jersey calf with a thick cream coat,

which he was scared of, in fact,
when it stumped over
the hummocked grass to greet us,

knots in its furry, flyblown ears.
We watched it take its milk, and now
he wants to make sure

of its mother and father, wants
to call them down from
the rapidly distancing hills, wants

to wrap the calf in a blanket,
press it safely under cover, the way
Peter and Mopsy are pressed

in their book, neat in their linen,
rush-lit bed: the way
his whole world, lately,

is honeycombed with dreams
of warm things, mice
about their tiny humid lives, spiders

snug in spouts. I stroke the soft
hot dome of his forehead, the furrow
where the line will come,

and say *yes* to the calf
in his unlikely blankets, the private
familial life of the flea. I say

all of them are warm enough, all
of them are tucked up now, listening
to their mothers' stories

as the globe turns to the enfolding
darkness, as we draw up
and stop the car in the dark.

Dumping the Christmas Tree

takes both of us, it transpires,
reeling to the park with our irregular
burden, strewing dead spines
like smoke from a censer. Afterwards,
wordless, we bash each other clear
of the needles and tinsel, Punch
and Judy in the freezing air.

What do they know of marriage –
these passers-by staring, these
thin joggers crunching hollow
ice in the puddles? You and I,
we have lived in Helsinki,
we have walked over
the dark rime of the sea.

Miscarriage, Midwinter

For weeks we've been promising
snow. You have in mind
thick flakes and a thick white sky;
you are longing to roll up
a snowman, to give him a hat
and a pebbly smile. We have ice
and I've shown you, under
the lid of the rainwater barrel, a single
spine forming, crystals pricked
to the delicate shape of a fir, but
what can I say to these hard
desolate flakes, dusting our path
like an industrial disaster?
It's dark, but I'm trying to scrape
some together, to mould just
the head of the world's smallest
snowman, but it's too cold and
it powders like ash in my hand.

Mendings

He is sitting in the bath,
telling the story where his ball
becomes a balloon, and after

long fugues involving aeroplanes,
tractors, oh, all the grand
detritus of space, bangs

into the moon and we mend it,
mend it, we have to get
moon glue. I'm squatting on the floor;

trying to let his voice, the net
of ripples in his hands, the line
of shine on his golden hair, thread

past my rocking legs, my arms
locked in temper.
The other night I told a friend,

a woman I've always liked,
that *happy ever after* is just
another room, and you're still

you in it; and now I'm wondering
even if that's true – but
she was saying she'd lost

her man, and when she smiled
I saw her teeth were old,
had that yellow sheen like Bakelite

or piano keys, and I thought
of her last eggs,
the womb staying empty, folded

like an evening purse, and anyway
on nights like these my heart
creaks on its fault lines like damp

in the marble veins of a fracture.
He's still talking.
He's saying the sun is in pieces,

and the stars are in pieces,
and we are mending them,
mending them, all of us

and the cat are mending them,
gluing them and now we are tired
and we're going home for a rest.

I gather up him up, his limbs
weighty and nacreous,
hold him close and damp in a towel.

From the window I show him
how, beyond the reflection –
where he is an angel leaning

out of a cloud – the winter
has widened the black of the sky.
There are the stars, and the moon,

unshattered, smudged tonight
like an ovum setting out
on its glamorous journey.

He puts his arms around my neck
when we walk down
the stairs, and they're steep

but that one time we slipped,
I sat down quick as déjà vu
and we were OK, OK. Now

my arms are full of him
and his head on my neck
is heavy and full. O moon glue,

sun glue, star glue. Surely,
across the universe,
the blocks of dark pulling always

randomly apart, I have seen
your glaucous threads
reaching, tenuously re-joining.

The Other Woman

I am running to meet her,
now, the girl who lives on her own,
who has in her hand the key to her own
hallway, her own bare polished stair, who
is clacking down it now, in kitten heels, swearing,
who is marching over envelopes marked with a single name,
who is late, can be late, sleep late, forget things,
who tonight has forgotten hat, gloves and
umbrella, and is running not caring
through the luminous rain.
What shall we say?

Shall I slip off
my coat and order cold wine
and watch myself sip it through
the long row of optics, arching my back
on the velvet banquette? And pick up the wit,
the moue of the mouth as we pass jokes like olives?
And say the right thing and stand up for my round,
tapping the bar with a rolled-up twenty,
tipsy, self-conscious, a girl,
a vessel of secrets, so
carefully held in?

Or down just one glass
and see stars and the whole
room go smeary, have nothing to say
and say all the same – apropos of nothing,
in the middle of everything – *You don't understand.*
What happens is someone slips from your side, someone
full-sized. Will she yawn, get her bag, start tucking
her fags in when I get out his photo,
say *Look, look how he's grown,*
all by himself, he has grown
to the size of my life?

Stance

Now I sit my child on the jut
of my hip, and take
his weight with the curve
of my waist, like a tree
split at the fork,
like lovers leaning out of a waltz.

Nothing is lost. I was never
one of those girls
stood slim as a sapling.
I was often alone at the dance.